SCIENCE SKILLS SORTED

LIFE CYCLES

ANNA CLAYBOURNE

W

FRANKLIN WATTS

LONDON • SYDNEY

Franklin Watts
First published in Great Britain in 2017 by The Watts Publishing Group

Credits
Series Editor: Amy Pimperton
Series Designer: Emma DeBanks
Picture Researcher: Diana Morris

Picture credits: Aaskolnick/Dreamstime: 24cl, 24cr. Ammzal12/Dreamstime: 11t. Ammzal13/Dreamstime: 11c. amphaiwan/Shutterstock: 8tlb, 8bl. Florian Teodor Andronache/Dreamstime: 12bl. Florian Andronache/Shutterstock: 12c. Best Vector 03/Shutterstock: 22bl. Best Vector 083/Shutterstock: 22ba, 22br. blickwinkel/Alamy: 20t. Catchtlght Lens/Shutterstock: 5cl. James Cavallini/SPL: 3br, 6cl. Paola Crash/Shutterstock: 3bc. Emi Cristea/Dreamstime: 21c, 29b. Custom Life Science Images/Alamy: 8tr. CyberKat/Shutterstock: 14c. Designua/Shutterstock: 10. Paul Fleet/Shutterstock: 4cr. Gallinago Media/Shutterstock: 20bl. Steve Gschmeissner/SPL/Alamy: 16t. Mark Higgins/Dreamstime: 10b. Hornbil Images/Alamy: front cover. Ian 2010/Shutterstock: 9b. Isselllee/Dreamstime: 13t. Amy Johansson/Shutterstock: 9t. Irina K/Shutterstock: 22tr, 29tc. Wolfgang Kaehler/Getty Images: 6t. Karen Kasmauski/Getty Images: 24b. V Kilikov/Shutterstock: 18b. Vitaly Korovin/Shutterstock: 23t. Alexander Kostyuk/Shutterstock: 20br. Komsan Loonprom/Shutterstock: 19b. Luayana/Dreamstime: 9c. Cosmin Manci/Shutterstock: 12ra. Brian Maudesley/Shutterstock: 27b. Mikadun/Shutterstock: 11b. Hiroya Minakuchi/Minden Pictures/FLPA: 22cl. mire/Shutterstock: 4bl, 4br. Monkey Business Images/Dreamstimes: 22cr. Monticello/Shutterstock: 19t. Josef Muellek/Shutterstock: 5b. Nagel Photography/Shutterstock: 4t. Liubov Nazarova/Dreamstime: 13b. Howard Nevitt Jr/Dreamstime: 25t. Tyler Olson/Shutterstock: 16b. Jurgen Otto: 15t. PeJo29/Dreamstime: 12bc. Kawin Phonkarn/Dreamstime: 18t. Piotreknik/Shutterstock: 27t. Plavevski/Shutterstock: 6b. Ra3rn/Dreamstime: 17t. Carlos Ramero/Shutterstock: 8br. Valentina Razumova/Shutterstock: 5c. Dr Moreley Read/SPL: 26t. Leena Robinson/Shutterstock: 7b. Sue Robinson/Shutterstock: 12br. Steven Roncin/Dreamstime: 24tc. Tui de Roy/Getty Images: 14t. Matteo Sani/Shutterstock: 8tl. Sarah2/Dreamstime: 12r. Science Photo Library: 16c. Andrei Shumskiy/Shutterstock: 7r, 25c, 29tr. Kenneth Sponsler/Shutterstock: 24tr. Sandra van der Steen/Dreamstime: 12cl. M S Sulaiman/Shutterstock: 5tr. Virgonira/Dreamstime: 12t. Vasily Vishnevskiy/Shutterstock: 1, 14b. Visuals Unlimited/Wim van Egmond/Getty Images: 5cra. Valentyn Volkov/Shutterstock: 5cra. wacpan/Shutterstock: 21t. Richard Whitcombe/Shutterstock: 26b. Daniel Wiedemann/Shutterstock: 4cl. Wildlife GmbH/Alamy: 10c. xpixel/Shutterstock: 4tc. Zou Zou/Shutterstock: 15b.

HB ISBN 978 1 4451 5149 6
PB ISBN 978 1 4451 5150 2

Printed in China

Franklin Watts
An imprint of
Hachette Children's Group
Part of The Watts Publishing Group
Carmelite House
50 Victoria Embankment
London EC4Y 0DZ

An Hachette UK Company
www.hachette.co.uk

www.franklinwatts.co.uk

MIX
Paper from responsible sources
FSC® C104740
www.fsc.org

CONTENTS

Worlds in **bold** can be found in the glossary on page 30.

WHAT IS A LIFE CYCLE?

A life cycle is the series of changes a living thing goes through in its life. It is born, grows up, and may **reproduce** or have babies.

Although plants and animals die, they leave behind the next **generation** – their babies or offspring. This means that each **species**, or type, of living thing can keep existing over a long period of time.

This huge oak tree began its life cycle as a tiny acorn.

Age 0
a killer whale baby, or calf, is born

Age 2
she stays with her mother for two years

Age 10
she has reached adulthood

Age 15
she finds a male orca to **mate** with

This diagram shows the life cycle of a killer whale, or orca.

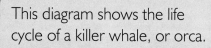

MAKING COPIES

When a living thing reproduces, it is making more living things of the same species. There are many different types of life cycle, and many ways for living things to reproduce.

A male and female elephant mate and the female gets pregnant. She gives birth to a live baby elephant.

Apple trees have flowers, which can grow into fruits. There are seeds inside the fruit that can grow into new apple trees.

This **amoeba** is a single-celled living thing. It reproduces simply by dividing in two.

Male and female Nile crocodiles mate, then the female lays eggs. The babies hatch from the eggs.

A strawberry plant can send out a stalk called a runner. The runner can grow into a new strawberry plant.

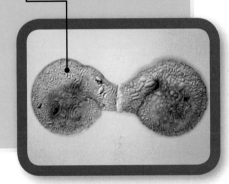

MATES OR NO MATES?

Some living things, such as elephants, have to mate to reproduce. This means a baby can only grow if a male cell joins with a female cell, making a new cell that grows into a baby. This is called **sexual reproduction**.

Others do not need a mate, such as the amoeba. It can reproduce by itself. This is called **asexual reproduction**.

HUMAN LIFE CYCLES

Humans are living things, and we have a life cycle too. Our species has existed for many thousands of years. Each individual human lives for around 80 years, and we keep our species going by reproducing and having babies. For example, there are about six generations between people who lived in Victorian times, and people who are alive now.

80-year-old

1-year-old

THE SCIENCE OF LIFE CYCLES

What is science? The word science means 'knowledge', so science is really just finding things out. Scientists study things in order to learn about them and find out facts. The things they learn can be useful in all kinds of ways.

These scientists are recording the size of a wandering albatross.

Studying and understanding the life cycles of living things is very important. It tells us a lot about life on Earth, and how it works. Besides understanding animals and plants, it helps scientists learn about things like dangerous **bacteria**, and how they breed and multiply.

Campylobacter bacteria cause food poisoning. Studying their life cycle can help us control them.

ENDANGERED SPECIES

Endangered species are living things that are in danger of dying out and becoming extinct. When a species is endangered, we can try to help it recover and increase its numbers. Studying its life cycle helps us to understand how to give that species the conditions it needs to reproduce.

For example, scientists have helped giant pandas – an endangered species – to have more babies.

WORKING SCIENTIFICALLY

In this book, you'll find a range of experiments and investigations that will help you discover how life cycles work.

To do experiments, scientists use careful, logical methods to make sure they get reliable results. The experiments in this book use four key scientific methods, along with an easy acronym to help you remember them: **ATOM**.

ASK

What do you want to find out?

Asking questions is an important part of science. Scientists think about what questions they want to answer, and how to do that.

TEST

Setting up an experiment that will test ideas and answer questions

Scientists design experiments to answer questions. Tests work best if you only test for one thing at a time.

OBSERVE

Key things to look out for

Scientists watch their experiments closely to see what is happening.

MEASURE

Measuring and recording results, such as temperatures, sizes or amounts of time

Making accurate measurements and recording the results shows what the experiment has revealed.

WHAT NEXT?

After each experiment, the What next? section gives you ideas for further activities and experiments, or ways to display your results.

FROM SEED TO SEED

Many plants reproduce using seeds. Here's how it works in a courgette plant.

male courgette flower (with **pollen** on **stamen**)

female courgette flower (with **stigma**)

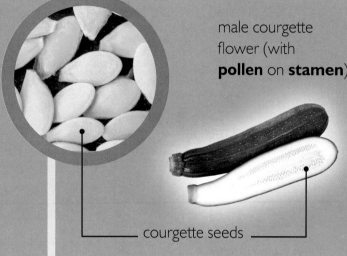

courgette seeds

pollen grain

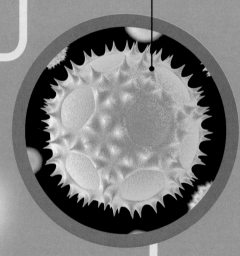

The courgette is a plant that grows from a seed and produces both male flowers and female flowers.

Male flowers release a yellow powder called pollen on the end of a stamen. Pollen is made up of male **reproductive cells** – the cells used for reproducing.

fruit

When the cells join, the female flower grows and turns into a fruit – a courgette. The seeds inside the courgette fruit can grow into new courgette plants.

The pollen cells can **pollinate** a female flower, meaning they join with the female reproductive cells in the flower. They can be carried there by the wind, or by **insects** that visit the flowers, such as bees.

SCIENCE EXPERIMENT:

GROW A PLANT FROM SEED

Pepper plants have 'perfect flowers'. This means the flowers have both male and female parts, and can pollinate themselves. You can watch a life cycle happening by growing a pepper plant from a seed.

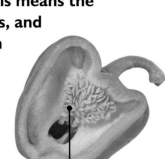

pepper seeds

Always wear gloves, and wash your hands after handling compost.

ASK

What does a seed do to make more seeds the same as itself? Will your plant complete a life cycle?

TEST

- Fill your pot with compost and make three small holes with a fingertip. Drop a seed into each hole and gently cover with soil.
- Keep your pot somewhere sunny and warm, like an indoor windowsill. Water every day to keep the compost damp.
- When plants appear, pull out the smaller ones to leave the biggest and strongest.
- When flowers grow, you can help the pollination process by using a soft brush or cotton bud to gently brush pollen from the male stamen onto the female stigma.

cotton bud

OBSERVE

Look for the first shoots appearing, and leaves and flowers growing. Watch how the flowers transform into fruits. Cut a fruit open to look for the seeds.

WHAT NEXT?

Can you grow a seed from your plant into a new plant? If you like growing plants, other good ones to try are tomatoes, carrots and sunflowers.

 ## MEASURE

How long does each stage take? How many flowers and fruits does your plant grow?

sunflower

EGGS AND BABIES

Some animals, like dogs, give birth to live babies. Others, like hens and crocodiles, lay eggs that babies hatch out of.

An egg has a shell or skin that protects the baby, and a supply of food for it to eat. Some eggs, such as turtle eggs, are soft and leathery. Others, like birds' eggs, have a hard shell.

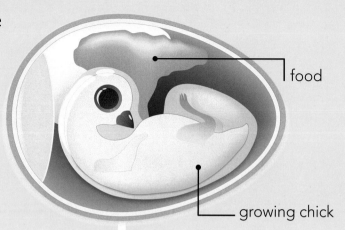

food

growing chick

This illustration shows an unborn baby bird growing inside its egg.

WHO LAYS EGGS?

All types of birds lay eggs. So do most **reptiles**, **amphibians**, fish and insects. However, some sharks, snakes and lizards give birth to live babies. So do some insects, such as **aphids**.

baby aphid

MAMMAL EGGS?

Most mammals have live babies. The only mammals that lay eggs are the **platypus** and the echidna.

echidna

SCIENCE EXPERIMENT:

EGG STRENGTH TEST

Birds' eggs have hard shells, which help to protect the chicks inside from being squashed when the mother sits on the eggs to incubate them. This experiment tests the strength of hens' eggs.

pointed end

rounded end

 Ask

How strong are hens' eggs?

 Test

- Crack each egg by tapping the middle sharply with a knife. Carefully pull the shell into two halves. Save the insides of the eggs in the food container to use for cooking.
- Carefully wash the shells with washing-up liquid and water. Leave them to dry.
- Put the tea towel on the ground and place your three more pointed eggshell halves on it in a triangle shape.
- Lay a firm hardback book on top.
- Now add more books, one by one, on top of the first book, until one or more of the shells breaks. Stand back so that the books don't hit you when they fall.

place the third shell under the centre of this end of the books

 Observe

Look at the eggs under the first book. Where does the book press on them?

 Measure

How many books can the eggs support before they break? Weigh the books to get an accurate measurement.

WHAT NEXT?

Try testing the more rounded eggshell halves. Do you get the same result? How do you think the eggs' dome shape makes them strong?

Some buildings have egg-shaped domes, like this cathedral in Florence, Italy.

METAMORPHOSIS

When a human, a cat or an aphid is a baby, it is basically the same shape as an adult – just smaller and cuter!

But think of a butterfly, a moth or a frog. Their babies look very unlike them – they are a completely different shape. They change a lot as they go through their life cycle. This changing is called **metamorphosis**.

Kittens resemble their parents.

BUTTERFLY LIFE CYCLE

This diagram shows the life cycle of a cabbage white butterfly, which goes through metamorphosis.

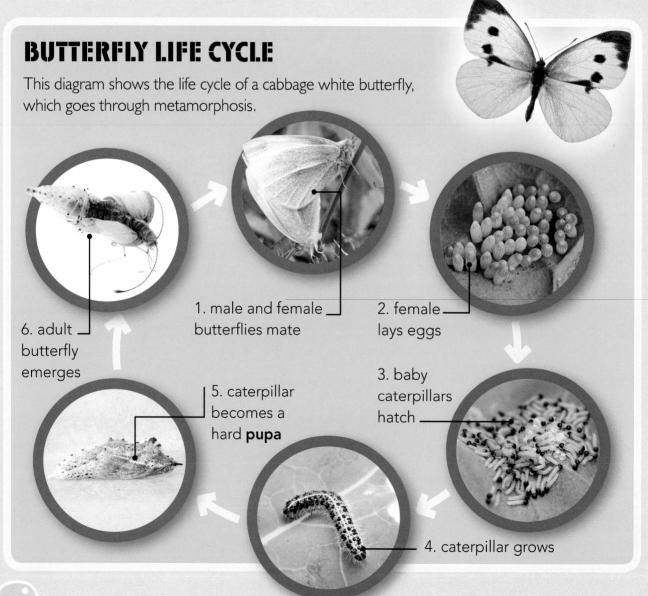

6. adult butterfly emerges

1. male and female butterflies mate

2. female lays eggs

5. caterpillar becomes a hard **pupa**

3. baby caterpillars hatch

4. caterpillar grows

YOU WILL NEED:

Container such as a large jar
Cardboard
Scissors
Sticky tape
Compost and gloves
Twigs and leaves

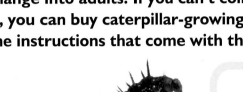

SCIENCE EXPERIMENT:

CHANGING CATERPILLARS

If you can collect caterpillars from a garden, you can watch as they change into adults. If you can't collect your own caterpillars, you can buy caterpillar-growing kits online. Follow the instructions that come with them.

Always wear gloves, and wash your hands after handling compost.

Ask

What happens to a caterpillar as it grows up?

Test

• Fill the bottom of your container with compost about 7 cm deep. Stand some twigs inside. Make a cardboard lid to fit the top, with some small air holes in it.
• To collect caterpillars, look on plants such as cabbages, fuchsias or fruit trees during the spring, summer and autumn months. If you find one, don't touch it, just pick the leaf or stem it is on. Put the whole thing inside your container. Collect up to 5 caterpillars of the same type.
• Use sticky tape to hold the lid onto your container. Put the container in daylight, but somewhere cool.
• If the food leaves start to go limp or brown, replace them with more of the same type.

Observe

Look at how the caterpillars feed, and how they change.

WHAT NEXT?

When the butterflies emerge, release them outside.

Measure

Measure how much the caterpillars change in size as they grow. After a caterpillar becomes a pupa, how long is it before the adult emerges?

Butterflies emerge from their pupae at a butterfly farm.

FINDING A MATE

Most animals use sexual reproduction. A male and a female get together and mate. The male gives the female his reproductive cells, or **sperm cells**. They join with her reproductive cells, or **egg cells**, so that babies can grow.

Male and female blue-footed boobies dance together before mating.

WHERE ARE YOU?

Animals use various methods to help them find a mate of the right species:
- Scent: some animals, such as emperor moths, can sniff out others of their own species.
- Colours and markings: these help animals recognise each other by sight.
- Calls or songs: some animals, such as songbirds, find a mate by following the sound they make.
- Movements: waving, head-bobbing or special mating dances are all used to attract a mate.

Male emperor moths use their feathery antennae to pick up the scent of females.

A brambling is a type of songbird. Male birds sing to attract a mate.

SCIENCE EXPERIMENT:

SENDING SIGNALS

This group experiment lets you test different types of signals and methods, to see how they help different species to spot each other.

Male peacock spiders display bright colours and wave their front legs to attract females.

YOU WILL NEED:

A group of at least 20 people
A large space
Paper and pens
Scissors
Sticky tape
Stopwatch

 Ask

How can species of animals find each other?

 Observe

How do the 'species' behave as they try to find their match?

 Test

- Split the group into two equal halves, leaving one or two people to observe the experiment.
- Design a range of signals that the pairs could use to find each other, such as:
  - Patterns or shapes drawn on paper and stuck to each person's top or forehead.
  - A special call, song, or sound to make, such as squeaking.
  - A type of movement to make with your arms or head.
- Separate the groups so they can't see each other. Give each person a signal to use, so that each signal will be used by one person in one group, and one person in the other group.
- Then jumble everyone together. Start the stopwatch and tell them to start using their signals to look for the other person that matches them.
- Once a pair find each other, they should go and line up so you can see the order it happened in.

Measure

Which signals worked best and fastest? How long did it take for all the pairs to match up?

WHAT NEXT?

What happens if you use just one type of signature, such as sound? Is it harder to find your mate?

Humans smile to let others know they are friendly.

15

DIVIDING BACTERIA

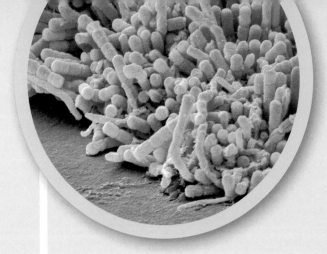

Bacteria are tiny, single-celled living things. They reproduce by dividing in two, then they grow and repeat the process. This is called **binary fission**. It's a type of asexual reproduction, meaning a bacterium does not need a mate to reproduce.

These are the bacteria that grow as plaque on your teeth, shown magnified by a microscope.

BINARY FISSION

'Binary fission' means 'division in two' and is the term that scientists use to describe how organisms, such as bacteria, reproduce asexually. This diagram shows how it works. Each new bacterium can divide again, making more bacteria. In this way, bacteria can multiply very fast.

As long as they have a supply of food, a small number of bacteria can soon become millions.

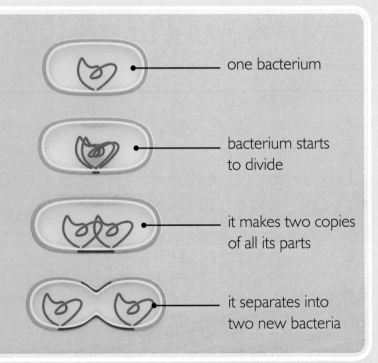

one bacterium

bacterium starts to divide

it makes two copies of all its parts

it separates into two new bacteria

BEATING BACTERIA

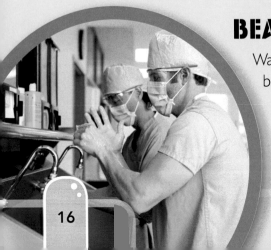

Washing your hands and cleaning your teeth help to kill harmful bacteria and stop them from multiplying. So does cooking and chilling food properly. Very high and low temperatures kill or disable most bacteria, but they can multiply fast at room temperature.

Surgeons have to wash their hands thoroughly to kill any bacteria before they can perform an operation.

Coloured blocks of modelling clay
A table to spread your model bacteria out on

SCIENCE EXPERIMENT:

MULTIPLYING MODEL

This model lets you investigate how quickly bacteria can multiply when they have a food source.

ASK

How can one bacterium reproduce and multiply to become many bacteria?

OBSERVE

Look at how the maths works. One becomes two, two become four, four become eight, and so on. Keep track of your bacteria carefully to make sure you divide them all at each stage.

TEST

- Take a large lump of clay or dough as a food source.
- Use a small piece of clay to make one sausage-shaped bacterium.
- Divide your 'bacterium' in half. Add more dough to make the halves into two new bacteria, each the same size as the first.
- Repeat the same process with your two new bacteria. Divide them both in half, and add dough to make all the new bacteria full-size. Keep going in the same way.

MEASURE

How many bacteria are there by the time you run out of food?

WHAT NEXT?

You could show what happens in each generation by drawing a diagram, like this.

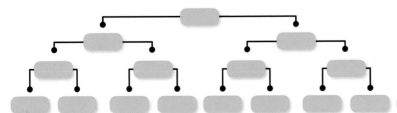

Can you make a graph to show how the bacteria increase over time? Can you calculate how many generations it would take to reach 1,000,000 bacteria?
(* See tip on page 32.)

BUDDING YEAST

Budding is a way of reproducing. During budding, a living thing grows a copy of itself from its body, which then breaks off. It's a type of asexual reproduction.

The hydra, a small creature that lives in water, can reproduce by budding.

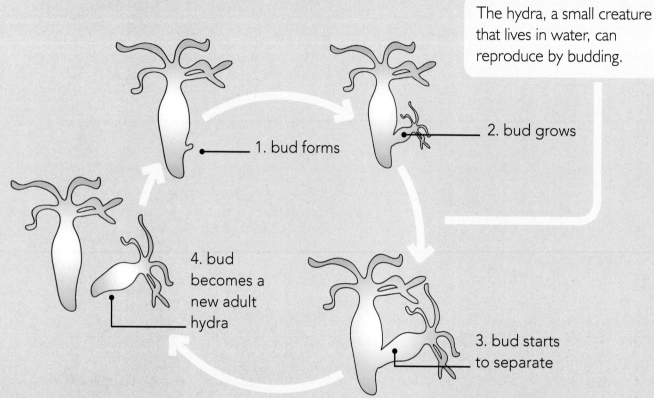

1. bud forms

2. bud grows

3. bud starts to separate

4. bud becomes a new adult hydra

YEAST

Yeast is a type of single-celled **fungus**. Yeast cells reproduce by budding.

When you add yeast to bread dough, the yeast cells feed on the sugar in the dough, and start budding. They are too small to see, but you can tell they are there because they release a gas called **carbon dioxide**. This is what makes the bubbles.

As yeast feeds and multiplies, gas bubbles form in the mixture.

Ask an adult to help with any baking.

SCIENCE EXPERIMENT:

RISING DOUGH

Make your own bread dough and see what happens when yeast buds and multiplies.

YOU WILL NEED:

1 sachet (7 g) dried yeast
300 g strong (bread) flour
190 ml warm water
2 tsp sugar • 1 tsp salt
Clear glass or plastic mixing bowl • Ruler • Tea towel
Oven, cooking oil and baking tray (optional)

baked dough

 Ask

What happens to yeast when it has food and water?

 Test

• Wash your hands before you start.
• Put the flour in the bowl, then add the other ingredients.
• Mix everything with your hands until you have a sticky dough.
• Put some extra flour on a table and turn the dough out onto it.
• Knead the dough for about 5 minutes, by folding it then stretching it out.
• Put the dough back in the bowl.
• Looking through the side of the bowl, measure how high the dough reaches.
• Cover with a tea towel and leave the bowl in a warm place for an hour.

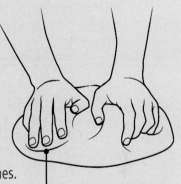
kneading dough

 Observe

Check the dough to see if it has risen. Tear it open to look for carbon dioxide bubbles inside.

 Measure

Measure the dough again after it rises. How much higher did it grow inside the bowl?

WHAT NEXT?

If you want to bake your dough, knead it again and shape it into a ball. Put it on a large, oiled baking tray, and leave to rise again for 30 minutes. Preheat the oven to 180°C and bake the dough for about 20 minutes.

Your body also contains yeast. This is a type of yeast that lives inside your intestines.

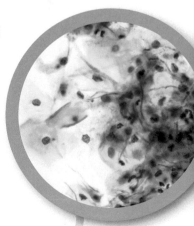

SPREADING OUT

As new living things are born, they have to spread out and find new places to live. For example, a young tiger will go off to find a new territory. Spiderlings (baby spiders) use threads of spider silk to float away or 'balloon' on the wind to find new places to live.

A spiderling waits for the wind to catch its silk thread and carry it away.

SPREADING SEEDS

Plants do this too. They **disperse**, or spread out, their seeds so that they will be able to grow somewhere far from the parent plant.

For example, some plants have parachute-shaped seeds that can easily blow away on the wind. Others are inside berries that birds or other animals like to eat. Later, the seeds come out in the animals' droppings, and start to grow.

These seeds have fluffy parts that help them travel on the wind.

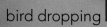

bird dropping

Birds fly long distances and spread seeds on their way in their droppings.

SCIENCE EXPERIMENT:

SEED DESIGNS

Design and make model seeds that you think will catch the wind. (They can be bigger than real seeds.)

YOU WILL NEED:

Modelling clay
Scissors • Paper •
Sticky tape • Tape measure
An electric fan
A selection of modelling materials, such as sewing thread, cotton wool, feathers, toy stuffing, etc

 ## Ask

What kinds of features help seeds to catch the wind?

Sycamore seeds have 'wings' that make them spin and fly sideways as they fall from the tree.

 ## Test

- Use modelling clay to make lots of small pea-sized balls, all the same shape and size. These are the basic seeds.
- Attach other materials to some of the seeds, such as paper shapes or fluffy threads, to help them catch the wind.
- Test your model seeds by switching the fan on, and dropping each seed into the path of the wind made by the fan.

WHAT NEXT?

If your fan has different speeds, try the experiment in 'light wind' and 'strong wind'. What other ways could seeds disperse? Can you find out about seeds that travel by water and seeds that disperse by exploding?

 ## Observe

How do the seeds move in the wind, and which travel the furthest?

 ## Measure

Measure how far each seed moved. Which were the best at wind travel?

Some plants, such as this burdock, have seed heads called burrs that are covered with tiny hooks. The burrs catch on animal fur or wool and get carried away.

21

GENERATIONS

A generation is the amount of time it takes for a living thing to grow up, become an adult, and reproduce, or have its own babies.

Of course, this varies, and in every species, there are some individuals that do not reproduce. However, on average, each species has a typical **'generation time'**. For example, in house mice, the generation time is only about ten weeks. In blue whales, it's much longer – about 31 years. Bigger animals tend to have longer generation times.

House mouse and babies

Blue whale and calf

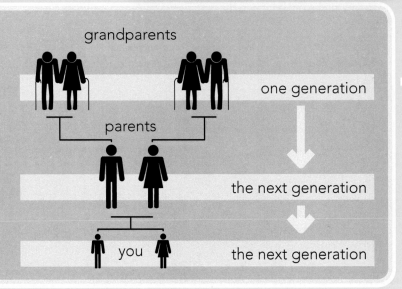

HUMAN GENERATIONS

Humans have generations too. Think about yourself, your parents, and your grandparents. You all belong to different generations.

grandparents

one generation

parents

the next generation

you

the next generation

SCIENCE EXPERIMENT:

GENERATION SURVEY

In this investigation, you collect data, or information, from real people, then study it to find something out. The aim is to find out the average length of a human generation.

 ASK

How long is a typical human generation?

 TEST

• To collect your data, you need to find women you know who have had children, such as relatives or friends' parents. Ask if they are happy to take part in your survey.
• If they are, ask them:
  – How old were they when they had each of their children?
  – What were the dates when their children were born?

 OBSERVE

Keep a record of your data by writing down all the answers, like this:

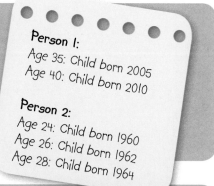

Person 1:
Age 35: Child born 2005
Age 40: Child born 2010

Person 2:
Age 24: Child born 1960
Age 26: Child born 1962
Age 28: Child born 1964

WHAT NEXT?

Can you find out more information from your data? For example, were generation times different long ago to more recently?

Can you research generation lengths for other animals, like giant pandas, crocodiles or bees?

 MEASURE

When you have asked everyone you can, count how many births you have in your list – for example, 20. Then add up all the mothers' ages at each birth. Finally, divide your result by the number of births. This will give an average generation time.

LIFE CYCLE MATHS

Most insect life cycles are short – a few days, months or years at the most. Periodical cicadas have extremely unusual life cycles. These small insects have a very long life cycle of either 13 or 17 years, depending on the species.

1. A cicada **nymph**, or baby, hatches from its egg and drops into the soil, where it spends either 13 or 17 years underground.

2. The nymph climbs out of the ground and up a nearby tree.

4. The adult cicada flies off and mates. A female cicada lays her eggs inside a tree branch.

3. An adult cicada emerges from the nymph.

ALL TOGETHER

The really strange thing is that in any one area, all the periodical cicadas of each species emerge at the same time. You won't see them for 13 (or 17) years – then, suddenly, they all come out at once.

Thousands of cicadas complete the stages of their metamorphosis to emerge as adults.

CICADA CALCULATIONS

This is a 'thought experiment', where you try to find something out by thinking about it and doing calculations. Can you figure out why periodical cicadas' life cycles are the way they are, and how they help them to survive?

YOU WILL NEED:

Paper and pens
A calculator

ASK

How does staying underground for 13 or 17 years help cicadas?

Male and female cicadas mate before the female lays her eggs.

TEST

Using a calculator to help you, create a 13 times table and a 17 times table next to each other on your paper. They represent the years when the cicadas emerge.

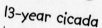

13-year cicada
1 × 13 = 13
2 × 13 = 26
3 × 13 = 39
4 × 13 =
5 × 13 =
6 × 13 =

17-year cicada
1 × 17 = 17
2 × 17 = 34
3 × 17 =
4 × 17 =
5 × 17 =
6 × 17 =

... and so on

OBSERVE

See how long you have to keep going before the same number appears in both tables.

MEASURE

How often would the two types of cicadas emerge in the same year?

WHAT NEXT?

It turns out that the numbers 13 and 17 have very different times tables that hardly ever match up. This means the different cicada species hardly ever emerge at the same time as each other – so they don't have to compete with each other for food.

HITCHING A RIDE

Some living things use others to help them complete their life cycles. If they do not help the other living thing in return, they are called **parasites**.

KILLER ZOMBIES!

The zombie ant fungus is a parasite that releases tiny seed-like **spores**. If one lands on an ant, it enters its body and grows into its brain. It controls the ant and makes it climb up a tall plant. Then the fungus grows out of the ant's head (which kills the ant), and releases more spores so it can reproduce.

New zombie ant fungi sprout from a dead ant's body.

HELPING EACH OTHER

Sometimes, though, both living things benefit. This is called **symbiosis**.

Clownfish live among the stinging **tentacles** of **sea anemones**, and are **immune** to the poison in the sea anemone's tentacles. This gives the fish a safe place to hide. In return, the fish defends the sea anemone from parasites and small predators.

A clownfish swims among a sea anemone's tentacles.

SCIENCE EXPERIMENT:

HOW BEES HELP

Honeybees have a symbiotic relationship with flowers. As they feed on nectar, they carry pollen grains from one flower to the next. Flowers can also be pollinated by the wind. This experiment explores the differences between types of pollination.

nectar

yellow pollen grains

 ASK

Do bees pollinate flowers better than the wind does?

 TEST

- Draw 20 flowers on the paper and cut them out.
- Tape ten flowers to the floor at each end of the room, in two groups of 5 – one group per team.
- Cut 10 tissue paper circles for pollen. Put them on the flowers at one end of the room.

Team 'Bees'   Team 'Wind'

- One team are Bees. They must pick up a piece of pollen, and put it on a flower at the other end of the room. Keep going until all the flowers have been pollinated.
- The other team is the Wind. They must try to blow their pollen onto their other flowers.
- Both teams start at the same time. Stop when one team has finished.

 OBSERVE

How hard is it to get the pollen in the right place by blowing?

 MEASURE

Which team finished first? How many flowers did the other team pollinate?

WHAT NEXT?

Some plants use wind for pollination. How do you think they make sure their pollen gets to the right place?

A male pine cone releases a cloud of pollen into the wind.

READING YOUR RESULTS

When scientists do experiments, they get results. Even if nothing happened as they expected, that is a result too! All results can be useful, but it is important to understand them. Here are some guidelines that scientists use to learn from their results.

USE A CONTROL

In the Seed Designs experiment (p. 21), the '**control**' items are the seeds with nothing attached. A control is a normal version of the set-up, without the thing that is being tested – in this case the attachments for catching the wind.

It's important that apart from the thing being tested, the control version matches the test version in every way. So the seeds must all be the same size, made of the same material, and blown by the same fan. Then you know that any differences in your results are purely down to the attachments.

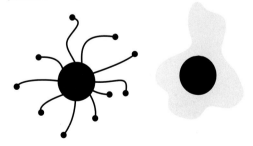

REPEAT AND VERIFY

An experiment may work well once, but what if that was a fluke? So that they can be sure of their results, scientists often repeat an experiment several times to **verify** their results.

CHECK FOR BIAS

If you're *really* hoping for an exciting result, it's possible you might accidentally-on-purpose 'help' your experiment along by ignoring something that doesn't fit with what you wanted. This is called '**bias**' and can happen without you even realising it.

OUTLIERS

What if you were conducting the Generation Survey experiment (p. 23), and your data showed that someone had had a baby when they were 120 years old?

You'd probably be quite surprised, as women usually stop being able to have babies in their 40s. In fact, hardly anyone lives to be 120 at all. This unusual result is called an **outlier**. Scientists have to check outliers carefully and work out why they have happened. For example, the most likely explanation for this outlier might be that you made a mistake when writing down your data, and put '120' instead of '20'.

KEEPING RECORDS

Writing down the details of each experiment and what the results were is essential for scientists. Not only does it help explain their work to others; it also means they can use results to look for patterns. For example, they might notice that white eggs are stronger or weaker than brown eggs.

MAKING MISTAKES

If you spot a mistake, start the experiment again. It would be an even bigger mistake to use the results from a badly run experiment.

However, if a mistake makes something interesting happen, you could set up a new experiment to test for that instead. Many important discoveries and inventions have been made this way. For example, hook and loop fasteners were invented by an engineer who noticed the tiny hooks on a burr stuck to his dog's fur. He realised that tiny hooks could be used to make a type of strong fastening.

GLOSSARY

amoeba A type of single-celled living thing.

amphibian A cold-blooded animal with a backbone. They usually breathe through gills as young and breathe air through lungs as adults.

aphid A small bug that sucks sap from plants.

asexual reproduction Reproducing alone, without needing a mate.

bacteria A type of microscopic single-celled living thing.

bias The tendency to look for what you want or expect to see from an experiment.

binary fission Reproducing by diving into two equal parts.

budding Reproducing by growing a smaller copy, which then breaks off and grows.

carbon dioxide A gas that is produced by some types of living things. Humans breathe out carbon dioxide.

control A standard version of something, used in an experiment to compare with the thing being tested.

data Pieces of information that are collected to be used for something.

disperse To spread out over a wide area.

egg cell Female reproductive cell.

endangered At risk of dying out and becoming extinct.

fungus A type of living thing that includes mushrooms, moulds and yeast.

generation A group that live at the same time. Their children are the next generation, their grandchildren are the generation after that, and so on.

generation time The time it takes for a species of living thing to complete its life cycle.

immune Not affected by something, such as poison.

incubate When a bird sits on eggs to keep them warm so they will hatch.

insect A small animal with a hard shell and six legs, and one or two pairs of wings.

mate Mating happens when a male and female living thing meet to join their reproductive cells together in order to reproduce.

metamorphosis Going through a series of changes during a life cycle; changing from one thing to another.

nymph The young or baby of some types of insects.

outlier A very unusual or unexpected result that is unlike the other results for an experiment.

parasite A living thing that uses another living thing to survive, but does not do anything in return.

platypus An egg-laying Australian mammal that lives on land and in water, has thick fur, and has webbed feet and a bill like a duck's.

pollen Male reproductive cells made by plants, which appear as a yellowish powder.

pollinate To join pollen cells with female egg cells in plants, in order to make seeds.

pupa A stage of development in the life cycle of some insects.

reproduce To have babies or offspring, so that a species can make copies of itself.

reproductive cell A cell used in reproduction.

reptile A cold-blooded animal with a backbone, such as a lizard, which has dry, scaly skin and usually lays eggs.

sea anemone A sea animal that has stinging tentacles and looks a bit like a plant.

sexual reproduction Reproduction in which two living things contribute male and female cells to make a baby or offspring.

species The scientific name for a group of living things that can breed and produce offspring.

sperm cell Male reproductive cell.

spore A type of tiny reproductive cell released by fungi and some other living things.

stamen The male part of a flower that carries the pollen.

stigma The female part of a flower that receives the pollen.

symbiosis Symbiosis happens when two species of living things work together and rely on each other to survive.

tentacles Slender, flexible body parts for holding food or prey.

verify To check and prove an experiment works.

BOOKS

Slimy Spawn and Other Gruesome Life Cycles
by Barbara Taylor (Franklin Watts)

Extreme Life Cycles
by Louise Spilsbury, (Franklin Watts)

Symbiosis: How Different Animals Relate
by Bobbie Kalman (Crabtree)

Straight Forward with Science: Life Cycles
by Peter Riley, (Franklin Watts)

*Explore Life Cycles! 25 Great Projects,
Activities, Experiments*
by Kathleen M. Reilly (Nomad Press)

Other books in this series:
Science Skills Sorted: Plants
Science Skills Sorted: Human and
Animal Bodies
Science Skills Sorted: Habitats
Science Skills Sorted: Evolution
and Classification
Science Skills Sorted: Rocks
and Fossils

WEBSITES

Brainpop: Scientific method
https://www.brainpop.com/science/scientificinquiry/scientificmethod/

School of Dragons: Scientific method worksheets
**http://www.schoolofdragons.com/how-to-train-your-dragon/the-scientific-
method/scientific-method-worksheets**

Science Kids: Biology
http://www.sciencekids.co.nz/biology.html

Education.com Life Science Activities and Experiments
**http://www.education.com/activity/
life-science/**

Cells Alive: Bacteria Divide and Multiply
http://www.cellsalive.com/ecoli.htm

INDEX

* **MULTIPLYING MODEL** tip: Use a calculator to make this much easier. Press 2, x, x, =. Then keep pressing =. The number should double each time from 2, to 4, to 8, to 16, and so on. Count the number of times you press the = button to get to 1,000,000 bacteria (including the first time you press it). This is the number of generations. Add 1 to your number to get the final number of generations, as you would have started with 1 bacterium, not 2.

SCIENCE SKILLS SORTED
These are the lists of contents for the titles in the Science Skills Sorted series:

PLANTS

What makes a plant a plant? • The science of plants • Working scientifically • Seeds • Plant defence • What plants need to grow • Surviving a drought • Water content • How leaves work • Helping nature • Flowers and seeds • Autumn colours • Cloning plants • Reading your results • Glossary and further information • Index

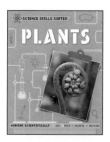

HABITATS

What is a habitat? • The science of habitats • Working scientifically • Wildlife habitats • Adaptations • Moving in • Blending in • Extreme habitats • Keystone species • How trees help • Balancing the numbers • Building the environment • Climate change • Reading your results • Glossary and further information • Index

LIFE CYCLES

What is a life cycle? • The science of life cycles • Working scientifically • From seed to seed • Eggs and babies • Metamorphosis • Finding a mate • Dividing bacteria • Budding yeast • Spreading out • Generations • Life cycle maths • Hitching a ride • Reading your results • Glossary and further information • Index

EVOLUTION AND CLASSIFICATION

What is evolution? • The science of evolution • Working scientifically • Evolution in action • Survival of the fittest • Finding food • Adapting to habitats • Winning a mate • Genes and generations • Classification • Sorting it out • Living relatives • The DNA key • Reading your results • Glossary and further information • Index

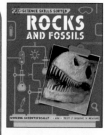

ROCKS AND FOSSILS

What are rocks, minerals and fossils? • The science of rocks and fossils • Working scientifically • Types of rock • Rocks and water • Minerals and crystals • How hard? • Weathering and erosion • Expanding ice • Making mountains • Volcanoes and earthquakes • How fossils form • Fossil puzzles • Reading your results • Glossary and further information • Index

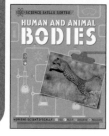

HUMAN AND ANIMAL BODIES

Humans and other animals? • Studying humans and animals • Working scientifically • Bones • Moving on land • Built to fly • Super streamlined • Sharp sight • Locating sound • Interesting smell • Teeth and beaks • Breathing • Unique individuals • Reading your results • Glossary and further information • Index